HENRY WILLIAM REDDICK
Florida State Archives

ELIZABETH M^cCORMICK REDDICK
Florida State Archives

Seventy-seven years in DIXIE

THE BOYS IN GRAY OF 61-65

By

H. W. REDDICK,

Price 50 Cents.

Published by H. W Reddick.

Santa Rosa. Washington County. Florida.

1910.

Foreword

Captain Henry W. Reddick is too well known to need any introduction from me. His life work and history are part of the history of Walton and Washington Counties, Florida, and the development of agriculture around the beautiful Choctawhatchee Bay.

His active participation in the Civil War is vividly illustrated within the pages of this book, and the history of that epoch-making struggle would not be complete if Captain Reddick had not put his experiences from the battlefield down in black and white, and thus made it possible to preserve it for coming generations.

Everybody interested in the history of the war should read this book, everyone whose ancestors struggled for victory on Dixie soil should read this book and keep it as a memento from the past; young men who don't know what war is should read this book and learn. It will teach a lesson those fancy volumes, written in perfume-laden parlors, by professional writers, at so much per word, never can teach. All honors to those professionals, but they have not had the experience of forced marches, starvation, exposure to rain, cold, hunger and bullets of the men who shouldered the musket and with their spirit fired by patriotism went to the front to fight battles for which they received no pay, nor ever expected to receive pay.

FOREWORD

They fought for principles, and if those principles were wrong, it was because the teachings had been led into wrong channels, not by the men of the field and forest but by the parlor professional who lived upon the toil of the men at work.

It is to be hoped that in the future the light of truth and justice will penetrate deep enough into the hearts of men, so that struggles like those portrayed in this little volume will not have to be repeated; that workers will not be arrayed against workers; brothers against brothers in deadly combat over something not tangible to either side, but that the words "united we stand" will be engraved in the hearts of men in a common united human brotherhood, for the peace and prosperity and happiness of all mankind.

A. P. BJORKLUND
FREEPORT, FLORIDA
SEPTEMBER 1910

Contents

I.	The Enlisting	5
	1864 Map of Pensacola and Vicinity	6
II.	The Battle at East Pass	11
	Map of Reddick's Civil War Travels	18
III.	Actual Service–The Kentucky Campaign	20
IV.	The Mississippi Campaign	36
V.	The Battle of Jackson, Mississippi	38
VI.	The Battle of Missionary Ridge	41
VII.	The Hundred Days Battle	47
VIII.	The Battle of July 22nd	51
IX.	The Battle of Franklin, Tennessee – The Worst Battle of the War	54
X.	The Battle of Nashville, Tennessee	64
XI.	Our Last Battle in the War	68
XII.	The Little Wonder That Never Was Satisfied	74
XIII.	Summary	76
XIV.	Civil War Poems	78

Chap. I

The Enlisting

When I first enlisted in the army of the Southern Confederacy, it was for one year—in 1861—our company was called the Walton Guards, on detached service, guarding East Pass [Destin, Florida] and the Narrows [Ft. Walton Beach], which had been bombarded by a United States gunboat.

The first flag I saw hoisted calling for volunteers to go to war was at old Eucheeanna, Florida. The ladies of the county hoisted that flag and marched around old Eucheeanna and made a direct appeal to each man in these never-to-be-forgotten words: "Go, boys, to your country's call! I'd rather be a brave man's widow than a coward's wife." To those loyal women is due the honor that sixty of us volunteered that bleak March day at old Eucheeanna.

In about a month we met again, organized and elected our company officers—Billie McPherson, Captain; Chas. L. McKinnon, 1st Lieutenant; H. W. Reddick [author], 2nd Lieutenant; A. B. McLeod, 3rd Lieutenant. We then appointed the hour for moving to the front, bade farewell to all who were near and dear to us, and designated the spot from which to embark, which was Alaqua Creek, just below Berry's little mill.

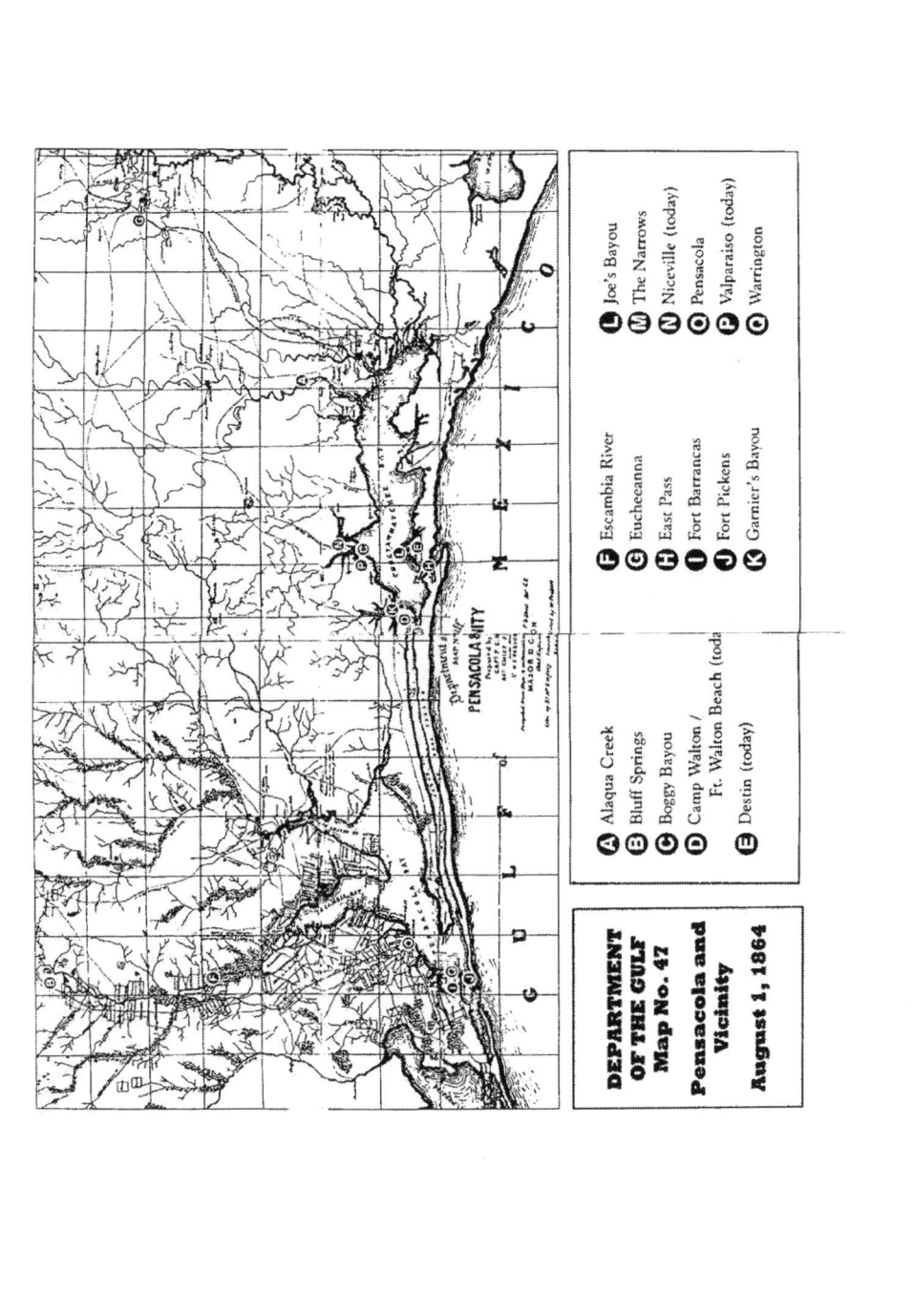

SEVENTY-SEVEN YEARS IN DIXIE

The night before our departure we met at a little cottage known as the Belcher Place, and I believe that nearly all the people of Walton County were present to bid us farewell. We danced all night, and as I was busying around it appeared to me that everywhere I went I found horses and buggies standing.

Next morning after breakfast, the program was to get on board the schooner *Lady of the Lake*, which was lying in the creek just below Berry's mill alongside the bank. We fell in line and marched down to the schooner. The crowds of people who had gathered to see us off followed us down to the bank, and when leaving time came the scene was one long to be remembered. Some were laughing, some were crying and some were making speeches. The order was given to get on board and we sailed down the Choctawhatchee Bay, arriving at Garnier's Bayou [Ft. Walton] next day, but stayed on board all night and until after breakfast next morning. The boys were feeding themselves and furnishing their own guns and ammunition and were in high spirits.

After breakfast a detail of twelve men was sent ashore to reconnoiter. They returned in about two hours, badly frightened, with the report that they had found a horse tied out in the woods. This was supposed to be a Yankee spy and the Captain gave the order, "Boys, all hands on deck! Leave your guns below and every man see that his shoes are well tied!" At least that is the story told on him.

Another detail was made, this time of twenty-four men, who were sent ashore and returned after a time with a man and a horse, but the man was not a Yankee spy, but old Bob Bell, who was charged with murder and was hiding from the sheriff.

THE ENLISTING

The next day we sailed on down to the Narrows where a site for the camp was selected, which was named Camp Walton. We soon had the camp ground and drill grounds cleared up and set to work building our houses, and in about a week we were well fixed and had a jolly good time.

For about two weeks as I remember we furnished our own rations and after that drew them from General [Braxton] Bragg at Warrington Navy Yard [Pensacola]. We had nothing but camp duty and drill to perform and were there for over a month before we were mustered into the service by an officer sent up by General Bragg for that purpose. We were mustered in for one year and signed the declaration of war.

Chap. II

The Battle at East Pass

During our stay at Camp Walton it was reported to Captain McPherson that a Yankee gunboat was lying off at East Pass on blockade duty and that she was landing troops there. This was reported to General Bragg at Ft. Barrancas [west of Warrington Navy Yard] and he instructed Captain McPherson to send a force over there and drive them off. Under these instructions Captain McPherson ordered a detail of forty men to go over there with the best guns we had, which were long-range muskets. When the men were lined up he gave them a little speech, and it must be admitted that some of the boys turned white, for it was known that this meant a fight and that at the time was a new business to them. However, they were ready to go, but when the matter was investigated, it was found that a part of the men who had the muskets were on picket duty, and so there were twelve of the force who were only armed with shotguns.

We had a long-boat with twelve long oars or sweeps and with these the boys pulled over to the head of Joe's Bayou [Destin] and, disembarking, marched two miles through the thick brush to the big red bluff opposite the pass where they lay in ambush watching the enemy. From this point they saw two boats leaving the gunboat, one some little distance in advance of the other. Our boys waited until they were within about 150 yards when the command was given to fire, and our boys poured in a volley which killed or wounded nearly every man in the boat, but the wind blowing off-shore drove the boat up on the island. A number of volleys were fired at the other boat but it was further off and not so much damage was done to it.

It was the Yankees' turn next and the gunboat turned her big guns loose in their direction, and Captain McPherson ordered a retreat to the boat and back to Camp Walton where the boys arrived without loss. We learned afterward that every man in the first boat except two was either killed or wounded, though some of our shotgun crowd told me that they saw their buckshot strike the water far short of the boat. I was on picket duty that day and did not get to go, though of course, the boys had my best wishes.

On their return, the Yankees got their guns on the beach and fired twenty-one shots at our schooner, *Lady of the Lake*, which was bringing up our supplies and was becalmed at the time and could not get out of the way. Lieutenants Chas. L. McKinnon and A. B. McLeod and eight men were on board of her at the time and, in addition, General William Miller, who at that time had no command, not having been mustered into the Confederate service. The men said that when the shots began coming, General Miller got up on the taffrail of the boat and shook his hat at them and gave them the rebel yell, but others of the men got down in the hold of the boat. Old Lee Ranier got behind the center case for better protection and when things were quiet would stick his head

THE BATTLE AT EAST PASS

up, but when another shot was heard would say, "Here comes another," and dodge down again. Captain Madison Reddick [author's brother—died at the Battle of Chickamauga] was in command of the schooner, and when a breeze sprang up, got out of range and then landed the supplies on the mainland side.

We had good equipment that we had brought from home and were enjoying ourselves finally until about eight or nine months after our enlistment when one morning we were startled by a cannon ball whistling over our heads. The Yankees had brought up two guns from Ft. Pickens [Pensacola] and had landed them on the outside beach and placed them behind some small hills on the islands just across the Narrows from us.

It was just at break of day, at which hour the rolls were called each morning and the men were forming in line and answering to their names, when they heard the roar of the gun and heard the shot whistle over their heads. It was a complete surprise and every man broke ranks and ran for his shack. I was not in the ranks, as I had been on duty all night and was in my shack sleeping and did not hear the first shot. The men were divided into messes of seven and eight men. Our brave little orderly sergeant was in my mess, and when that first shot was fired, made for the shack where I was sleeping and yelled that the Yankees were shooting at us and for me to get up quick. I thought that he was teasing me and while we were talking the second shot came, the ball going through our house near the top and just over my head. There was no more talking. I jumped up and began looking for my pants and shoes, which I had a hard time finding, though I did so at last and ran outside, and about that time the third shot came and went through our houses. All the men were running and dodging in every direction.

I had not yet gotten into my pants and shoes, and the cannon balls were coming thicker and nearer every minute. I finally got out of the range of the guns and got my pants and shoes on, and the next thing I heard was Captain McPherson calling for Lieutenant Reddick to help get the men into line. After some time we rallied the men and got them in line behind the little mound between us and the water. The Yankees evidently could hear our voices, for they dropped a cannon shell just behind our ranks, which caused a general stampede, every man breaking for the hammock in our rear and only a short distance away. There we rallied again and formed our line in the thick woods in an old road that led northward.

There Captain McPherson made a little talk to the men and ordered every man who would not risk his gun to step one pace to the rear, an order that about one-third of the company, those armed only with old shotguns, obeyed. Just as they stepped back, the Yankees got our range again and sent another shell over our heads, and such a scattering there was. Every man for himself for over two miles when we were brought up by the waters of Garnier's Bayou, all except two or three who were reported to have swum the Bayou and I know that two or three men did not report for three weeks afterwards.

We camped on the bayou that night, the Captain placing a heavy guard around the camp. During the night the guards stationed below and above Camp Walton reported to Captain

THE BATTLE AT EAST PASS

McPherson that the Yankees were crossing the Narrows in small boats, but the report proved to be false, though it frightened the whole community very badly at the time.

Next morning a small detachment was sent up in a small boat to meet the schooner *Lady Ann* commanded by Captain Baker, who was bringing our mail over the Bay, and to direct him to bring the *Lady Ann* into Garnier's. He arrived the next day and we were ferried across the bayou and marched some seven miles through the woods to Boggy Bayou [Valparaiso/Niceville], when we struck camp again and remained some three weeks, our commander in the meantime notifying General Bragg of what had happened. His orders were for us to return to Camp Walton and hold that place at all hazards.

These orders were obeyed, but we had a taste of war. After our panicky retreat Captain McPherson had ordered all our houses burned, and when we got back to the old ground we were without shelter of any kind for about three weeks when General Bragg sent us some tents and two thirty-pound cannons. One was mounted upon a mound near the water's edge and pointed towards the little hill on the island behind which the Yankees had placed their guns when they fired on us in camp. The other never was mounted, and when we evacuated the camp it was buried about fifteen paces from the water's edge.

The engineer who superintended the mounting of the gun was Dr. Chas. McKinnon, sergeant of our company. Not a man nor an officer of our company of ninety-two men had ever fired a cannon or stood near one when it was fired and some of them had never seen or heard one. Some of the men were drilled in the artillery tactics but were never called upon to exercise their knowledge.

A short time after this we received orders from General Bragg to report to the officers in command at Pensacola who sent a steamboat up to a point about thirty-five miles below our camp, and mules and wagons were sent by road to haul our equipage down to that point. Our baggage was packed up and we marched the thirty-five miles to the boat, which took us to Pensacola. About three weeks later we had orders to cook up two days' rations, and I was sent with a detail of fifty men up the [Escambia] river to Bluff Springs [Florida], about one hundred miles by water, with instructions to obstruct the river behind us, which we did by cutting cypress trees and falling them into the river. The rest of the command marched to Bluff Springs destroying the railroad

THE BATTLE AT EAST PASS

as they went. We rejoined them there and were with other companies organized into the First Florida Infantry. We did not stop here long, but during the time, many of our men were sick and some of them died. Amongst these I remember Calvin Lewis, Johnnie McDonald, Willie and Jessie Rooks, who were members of our company (E).

Reddick's Civil War Travels

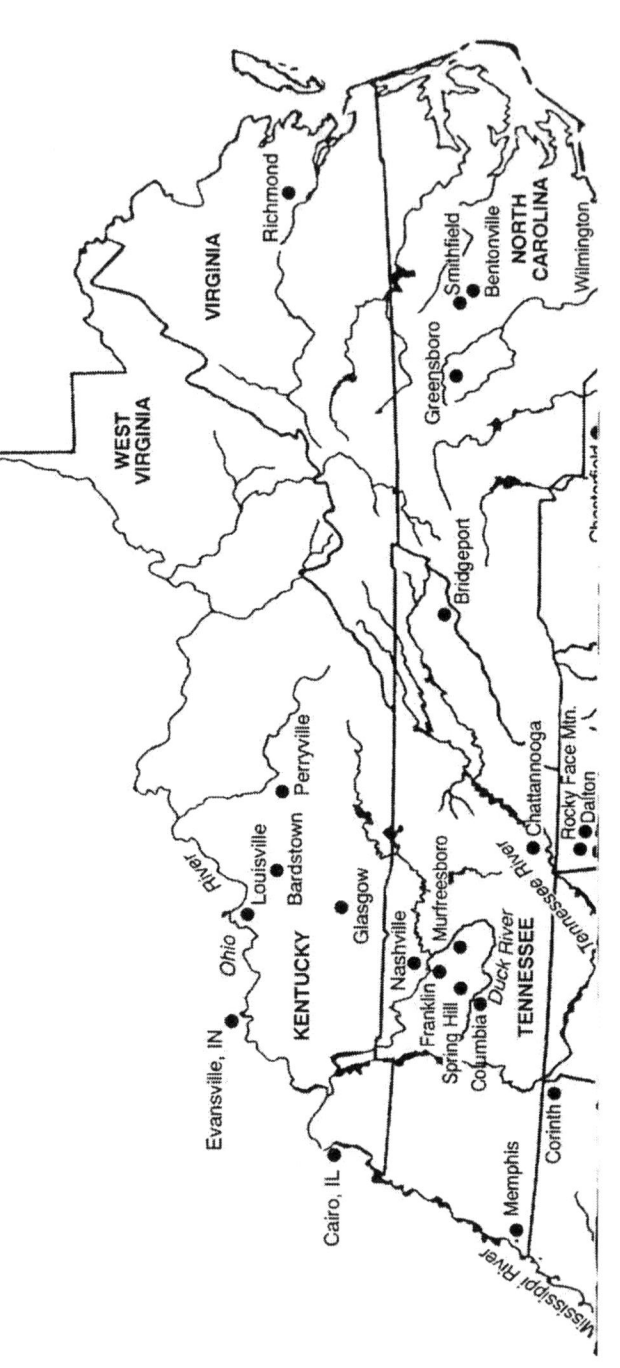

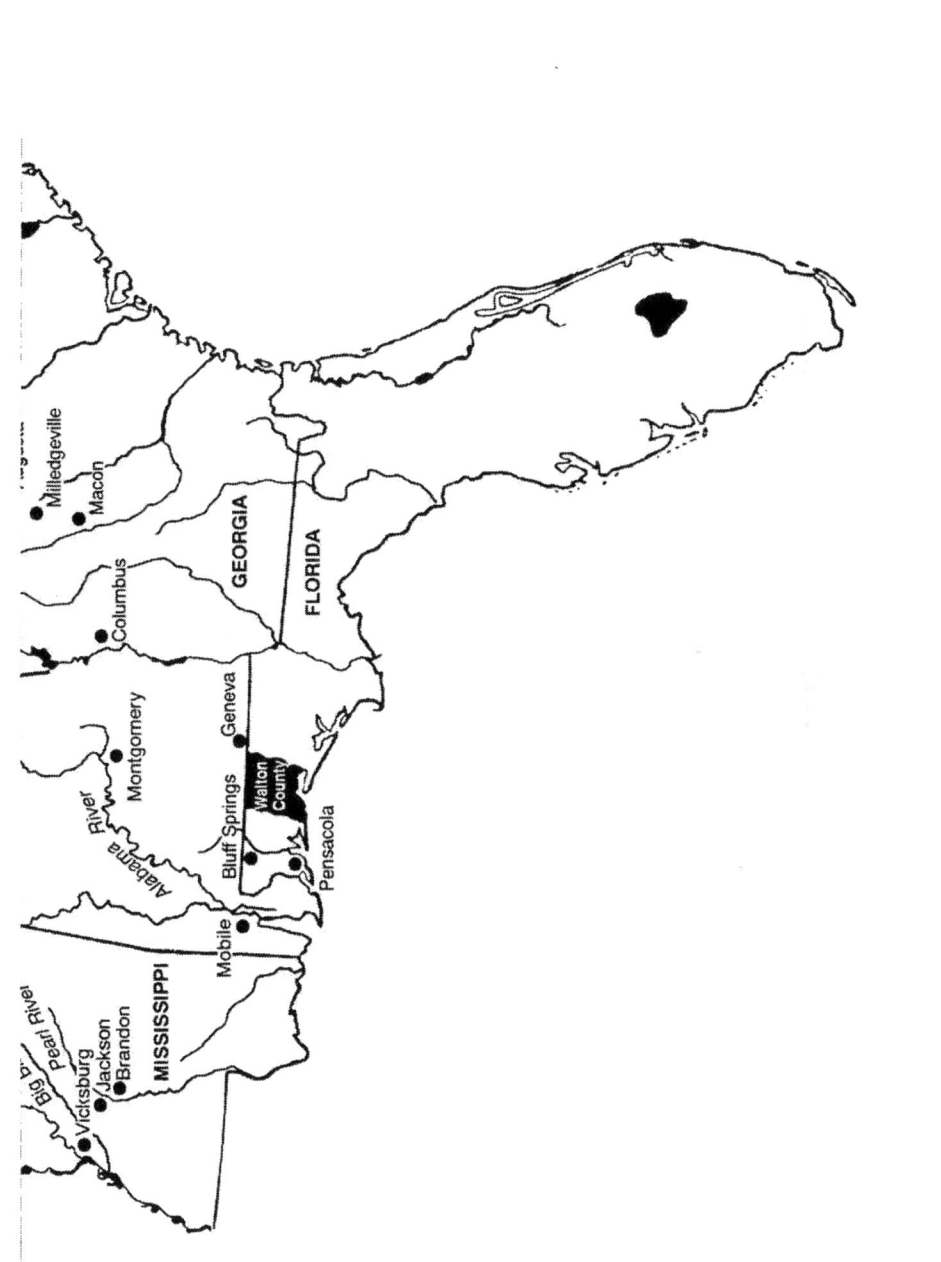

Chap. III

Actual Service – The Kentucky Campaign

OUR next move was to Chattanooga, Tennessee, where we saw the first of what the officers called actual service. The first thing was to deposit all our surplus baggage, and that meant everything we could not carry on our backs, with a baggage master. We had a lot of such things as feather pillows, quilts, cooking utensils, etc. We were told that we would get it all back when we returned from Kentucky, but never heard of it again. That was the last of it.

Our next move was to cross the Tennessee River, which we did at night. We were ordered to go up and draw rations; flour and bacon, but no salt, was what we got. The next morning we started on Bragg's raid into Kentucky. The first day's march was a short one and the first night we baked our hoe-cakes on flat rocks. Some of the boys used their ram-rods, rolling the leathery dough around them and holding them over the fire to do the baking. There was no salt or grease in them and they stuck without any trouble. The cook wagons were behind and there was no telling when they would come.

The next march was over the Blue Ridge, three miles to the top, four miles across and three down to the valley on

ACTUAL SERVICE – THE KENTUCKY CAMPAIGN

the other side. The road up was in the shape of a rail fence, and it took from ten to fifteen men to the wagon to help the mules up the hill with their loads.

It was on the mountain that Henry Wright and myself shed a part of our load. I threw away a good feather pillow and two quilts and I think Henry got rid of about the same amount of stuff. I carried only one quilt and the best suit of clothes I had, my knapsack and old haversack, and in it but very little rations.

The next place was at Murphreesville (Murphreesboro) [Tennessee – July 13, 1862], where General Bragg placed some of his heaviest guns in position to command the town and demanded its surrender, which was granted. The Yankees surrendered six thousand prisoners, several cannons besides a quantity of small arms and ammunition.

After a short stay here, we started for Bardstown [Kentucky], with General Bragg hustling us through on a forced march—we on foot traveling almost as fast as the cavalry could go. General [Don Carlos] Buell's [Federal] army was marching on a road about ten miles west of us and parallel with us and for several days we were in this position, and it was there that General Bragg missed his opportunity for victory in not giving battle. We reached Bardstown without any fighting, and the Confederate flag was planted on top of the courthouse.

Before this, however, Captain McLeod, Captain Coleman, Lieutenant Nicholson, two lieutenants from Arkansas, and myself had gotten our feet so severely blistered that we could not march and were given permission to fall out of the ranks and get along the best we could. Our feet were so sore that we could hardly march at all, and for two days we hired an old farmer with a two-horse team to haul us. We had gotten so far behind that we could not draw rations and had to depend upon what we could get to eat along the road. We drove up to the hotel in a little town called Glasgow [Kentucky], and expected to get a good dinner, as we were very hungry, so we thought Lieutenant Nicholson went in to order dinner for seven, but soon came back with the word that there was nothing there. The landlord said that General Bragg's army had just passed through and cleaned up everything there was to eat in the town, but he said that if we would go down the pike about two miles and call at a large two-story white house, we could get dinner because a rich widow lived there who had plenty.

We struck out for that place which we reached in due time, and the crowd put it to me to see if we could get dinner and I went in. I had to go back to the kitchen before I found her, but when I did and told my wants she agreed with the best humor to get dinner for us, but said we would have to wait until it was cooked which would take about half an hour. The boys were glad when I told them of my success, for they were hungry enough to have eaten up the whole place. The owner of the team unhitched his team and joined us at the table while we were eating the splendid dinner the lady had prepared for us. We were enjoying the dinner as only hungry men can enjoy such a meal when we heard the sound of horses coming down the pike from the direction of Glasgow.

This did not particularly alarm us as we had just come from that direction, and the landlady suggested that it was probably her boy Johnnie, which it proved to be, for a few

ACTUAL SERVICE – THE KENTUCKY CAMPAIGN

moments later he rushed into the dining room exclaiming, "Mama, the Yankees are in Glasgow."

At the words we jumped up from the table, but she urged us to sit down and finish our dinners saying that possibly Johnnie was mistaken, and we turned to our dinner again, but had hardly seated ourselves before we heard the sound of a large force of horsemen coming down the road, and, to tell the truth, the Yankees were at the gate before we could get out of the house. Some of the boys suggested that we go upstairs and others that we go out the back way, and in the haste to get away we divided, three going upstairs and three out the rear. Captains McLeod and Coleman and Lieutenant Nicholson went upstairs and under the beds, where the

Yankees found them and dragged them out by the heels. Myself and the Arkansas lieutenants made our way for the woods about two hundred yards away, having to climb over two fences on the way, or rather falling over them. The Yankees saw us before we got to the woods and commenced firing at us, but with no other effect than to increase the speed of our leg action. As we fell over the second fence we fell down and watched the Yankees march our friends off and saw the old farmer drive off with all our baggage.

We had left our hats in the house and were bare-headed. We kept in the woods for two days and one night and with nothing to eat. It seemed to us that every road was full of Yankees. The second night we went to a farmhouse and got something to eat, and on the morning of the third day caught up with the army and joined our command.

The army stopped at Bardstown for some time, and our Florida brigade was placed on picket duty some six miles out on the Bardstown and Louisville Pike, and while there we got pumpkins to eat. During this time I was taken sick with a severe fever and was sent to the hospital in Bardstown, where I found a good many of our soldiers laid up for repairs.

It was only a few days before General Buell commenced advancing and Bragg fell back to Perryville [Kentucky – October 8, 1862] without offering any resistance, leaving the sick to be taken prisoners, and among them was Captain McPherson and myself. At Perryville Bragg joined General Kirby Smith with about twelve thousand men and made a stand against Buell, and our boys who were wounded and captured there said that while Bragg put up a good fight, Buell outnumbered him so badly that he had no chance. My

ACTUAL SERVICE – THE KENTUCKY CAMPAIGN

room was in the third story of the Female Academy, which was used for a hospital, and it fronted on the street so that I saw Buell's army as it passed through, taking nearly two days to do so. I counted 110 flags and estimated one thousand men to the flag. The wounded captured at Perryville were sent to the hospital at Bardstown, and there many of them died.

We fared very well while our army was in Bardstown, but after it was captured by the Yankees things were bad indeed. While our army was there the ladies visited us and did everything they could for us, but when the Yankees came in, this was not allowed. If it had not been for the Sisters of Charity we would have fared much worse. They did everything they could for us, and I for one will never forget their kindness.

It was about three weeks before I was able to walk around any. One time after I got up, Captain McPherson and I walked down in the town, which was full of Yankees. I had a very fine gold hunting case watch that I had when I enlisted and of which I thought a great deal. A big, double-jointed Yankee stepped up to me and asked to see my watch. I took it off and handed it to him and he put it in his pocket and walked off, saying that he would see me again, which he never did, but I often wish he had.

After Captain McPherson and myself got strong enough to walk, we were paroled. We wanted to go south, of course, but this the Yankees would not allow, but gave us permission to go north as far as we wanted to. About a week after this we were sitting in the sun one day warming ourselves and talking of home and homefolks. A fine carriage drove up and a well dressed man got out and, seeing by our uniforms that we were Confederate soldiers, introduced himself as Reverend Mr. Beardsley of the Methodist Church. He assured us of his sympathy and gave us two bottles of fine Catawba wine which he had in his carriage. He offered to take us to Louisville [Kentucky], but we told him that we did not have any Yankee money. He then said that he would take us to the United States Hotel there, and that there were plenty of Southern people who would see that our board was paid.

We told him that we would be glad to go, and he said for us to be ready at noon and you may be sure that we were. He was on time and getting in his fine carriage behind his high-stepping horses, we were soon hitting the rocky pike in the direction of Louisville where we arrived soon after sundown. On the way we passed through a large cemetery, and all along the road near the town Yankee pickets were posted thick.

We drove up to the United States Hotel where the preacher left us for a few moments while he arranged for our rooms, which were on the third story. We remained there for three weeks and in that time wanted for nothing. I think we only saw him once after this, however.

This was some days later when he gave us an invitation to go with him to visit one of his old lady friends and church members. We accepted provided he would go with us, which he agreed to do and called for us that night at seven. Going down the street it seemed to me that I had never seen buildings so large and high. At the steps of the house where we went, we were met by four or five young ladies and invited into the sitting room, and soon the old lady came in, but her name I do not remember. She was a great talker and

ACTUAL SERVICE – THE KENTUCKY CAMPAIGN

soon got started. She said that she had always wanted to see a Confederate soldier and this was her first opportunity.

I think that she had the same idea about us that some of the people in the far South had about the Yankees. I remember once when working on the roads near Sugar Valley in Georgia, being asked by some young ladies if I had ever seen a genuine Yankee soldier. When I said that I had, they asked what they looked like and if they were blue. I told them no, but that they wore blue clothes and that we called them "blue-bellies" when by ourselves, but when on picket near one another they called us Johnny Rebs and we called them Mr. Yanks.

During our visit with the young ladies that night we enjoyed ourselves to the utmost, though I believe Captain McPherson enjoyed himself better than I did. The young ladies were well-educated and used big words that I did not know the meaning of, though he did, for he was a young lawyer who had enlisted from our county. I think that his grammar helped him out that time. We remained until about ten o'clock when we were escorted back to the hotel by Mr. Beardsley, and this was the only visit we made while in Louisville.

Both the Captain and I were great smokers and used lots of matches, and on our return to the hotel I suggested that we go into the office, which was on the ground floor, and ask for some matches. The office was full of Yankee officers, and we crowded through up to the desk and asked for some matches. The clerk soon brought us a box which we did not open until we reached our room, and when we did so we found a twenty-dollar bill tucked in on top of the matches which the clerk had placed there for us.

SEVENTY-SEVEN YEARS IN DIXIE

One morning after this we walked down the street and on every side people would stop and stare at us. We went into a dry goods store, wearing our uniforms with the brass buttons on which was stamped the motto, "United We Stand," which marked us as Confederate officers. The proprietor was a Southern sympathizer and was very glad to see us, and when we left he gave us fourteen yards of Confederate gray cloth for new uniforms, which we managed to smuggle through the lines and bring back to Dixie with us.

The next morning the Captain went down and got our bill, which was Kentucky State currency, changed. After that we would send out by the boys from the street who often came up to see us, for such things as we wanted to eat, and they always treated us right and were honest with us.

Our meals were our worst trouble. We had plenty to eat and three meals a day, but the dining room was on the first floor and was always full of Yankee officers. The tables were round, seating four, and we always tried to get one where there was no one else. Sometimes we were successful, but often Yankee officers would come to our table and sit and eat. Some of them were agreeable, while others were rude and insulting, cursing the South and the people as rebels and traitors. Dinner was from twelve to three but we always ate as quickly as possible and went back to our rooms. We were there three weeks to a day when one morning an officer came up to our room, seemingly very much pleased at something, and after a few words said, "Gentlemen, I have orders for you to report down to Colonel Farrell's office at the prison."

ACTUAL SERVICE – THE KENTUCKY CAMPAIGN

Thinking that we were to be sent South the Captain and I were highly pleased, and asked if we should take our little grips with us, and he told us to do so. We were ready in a few moments and went downstairs where we found a hack with two soldiers as guards with fixed bayonets. We were ordered in the hack with little ceremony and, obeying, were driven about two miles to Colonel Farrell's headquarters and given orders to report to him in his office. When we entered he was seated at his desk, writing, and when we said good morning, did not even look up. Presently he gave an order for the sergeant to take our description, which he did, measuring our heights and around us with a tape line and making a note of our complexions and hair, etc. He next searched us, going through our grips and over our persons, taking everything except our clothes, even to a few apples we had. The sergeant was then instructed to take us down to the prison, which he did, and when we reached the gate, told us to walk in. This cut our feathers considerable, but we felt better when we found so many of our boys there. All told there were about sixteen hundred Confederate prisoners there. Colonel Farrell was about the most contemptible specimen I have ever met and why he was so mean to us I have never been able to understand, even taking our apples and pocket knives. For three weeks we had been at the hotel mingling with the Yankee officers every day, eating in the dining room and often at the same table, and yet when they sent us down to the prison we were sent with two armed guards.

The prison fare was considerable of a change to us. At the hotel we had plenty, but here we got a piece of bakery bread, about as wide as three fingers and as long, and a piece of fat boiled pork about two-thirds that size twice a day with half a tin cup of coffee in the morning. The table where our rations were set out for us was in another room. We passed through a door in single rank and marched by the table, picking up our bread as we went along and then out through another door. A strong guard was placed in the room to see that no one got more than his share. The weather was very cold and we were allowed but one heater to one hundred men and a very short allowance of wood.

We were kept here about two months, when one morning we were ordered to fall in preparatory to going South, and we were glad indeed to hear it. After we fell into ranks at the gate, an officer told us that we would be marched directly through the city and that possibly handkerchiefs would be waved at us from some of the windows or galleries and warned us that any one cheering them would be shot down on the spot.

We were formed in single rank formation, our blankets and knapsacks searched, and then formed in ranks eight deep and were marched through town to the river bank, a distance of about two miles. Here the steamer *Mary Miller* was waiting for us. Coming through town we could see handkerchiefs waving at us from nearly all the larger buildings. While we were standing on the bank one of our boys saw a handkerchief waving at his part of the ranks and hallooed for Dixie and the guard shot him down like a dog. Sixteen hundred and eleven of us were marched on board, and we started down through the locks of the Ohio [River] on our way, as we thought, to Dixie. The next day, a good distance down the river and near the town of Evansville on

ACTUAL SERVICE – THE KENTUCKY CAMPAIGN

the Indiana side, we ran aground on a sand bar, and as many of the prisoners as was necessary to lighten the boat were sent ashore in small boats. About three o'clock the *Mary Miller* was afloat again and we were marched back on board, and our journey was resumed. The next night when we were near Columbus and it was dark as pitch, I was asleep when a cannon ball whistled over the boat. By the time I got awake another one came along and everything was excitement. Some of our men thought that the Yankees were trying to sink the boat with us prisoners on, but we soon found out that the Captain had given the wrong signal and this had brought the fire on us from the Fort. We remained there until the next morning, when the Captain was arrested and taken ashore and another officer placed in charge.

He was a hard case and treated us "traitors," as he called us, as mean as he possibly could. We left about nine o'clock and steamed on down to the mouth of the Ohio to Cairo [Illinois], where we landed and marched a short distance up the street, where we were ordered into company front, and every prisoner who had a blanket marked "U.S." or a blue overcoat was directed to step to the front and put these articles on the ground. This brutal order left about half of us without either blanket or overcoat and the weather was bitter cold. We were then marched about two miles to an old barracks and placed under Negro guards, in whose camps were a number of cases of smallpox.

For two months we were kept here on short rations and the sufferings of all our men—particularly the large number of those who were still suffering from the wounds received at Perryville—were terrible. Little to eat and nothing to either sleep on or cover with. Go to bed hungry and cold and get up the same way, Cairo prison will always be remembered by me. Little did we think when we enlisted for three years for the war and left all who were dear to us that this was what we were coming to. Many and many were the desires that were expressed to get back home to wives, mothers and sweethearts.

One day about fifty of us old rebel prisoners were sitting out in the sun warming ourselves when a strange officer came up and directed us to be ready at two o'clock to go South. This news was so good that it put new life in every one of us, and we were ready before the hour. The gates were thrown open and we were marched down to the [Mississippi] river and got on board a big three-deck river steamer by the name of *Mary Downing*, and started again for Dixie. There were over sixteen hundred of us on board and over five hundred of those were wounded from Perryville. We started about four o'clock with an old ironclad steamer just ahead of us. I think that we were nineteen days on board of her making the trip. We had plenty of rations, good bacon and flour and coffee, but the trouble was that we had no place to do any cooking. We ate the meat raw and only occasionally could we get the firemen to allow us to make coffee on the boilers.

One deck of the steamer was given up to the wounded and a visit there was enough to sicken anyone. The poor boys suffered horribly, there was no way nor anyone to dress their wounds, and fifty-five of them died before we reached Vicksburg [Mississippi]. When one died his body would be rolled up in his blanket and nailed up in a rough pine box. The steamer would slow down for a few minutes and the

ACTUAL SERVICE – THE KENTUCKY CAMPAIGN

body would be taken ashore and buried on the bank of the river.

One day as we were steaming down the river we were fired on by a force of about five-hundred guerrillas from the Missouri side. They had dismounted and run down to the river side and turned loose two or three volleys at us. The ironclad ahead of us rounded up and fired two or three of her big guns in their direction and they retreated up the hill in double-quick time and in bad order. I do not know whether they were firing at us prisoners or the Yankee guards. None of our boys were hurt, though a good many of the bullets struck the wheelhouse, and I heard that one of the guards, who was standing aft, was killed. All that we rebs could send back at them was our old charging yell.

Soon after this our boat got aground and stayed three days. Our next excitement was when the boat got afire and came near burning up, together with her captain. He let his bedding catch fire one night about ten o'clock, and a number of our Confederate officers ran up and threw the bedding overboard and came near throwing the captain with it. The army officer in command seemed to think it a good joke on the captain of the boat.

There were about three hundred Confederate officers on the boat. When we reached Memphis we made a stop of about three hours, but the steamer was not allowed to land but was kept off some thirty yards from shore. A large crowd of ladies was on the banks and they had apples and cigars for us but were not allowed on board to give them to us, but they would tie small rocks to cigars and throw them aboard. Some reached us and others fell short and fell in the river.

SEVENTY-SEVEN YEARS IN DIXIE

About a dozen of our boys got on the upper deck and sang the old southern songs in spite of the repeated orders of the Yankee officers to stop. The ladies on shore would wave their handkerchiefs and throw kisses to us, that is, to those they knew, for there were a good many on board who had friends and relatives on shore but the best they could do was to exchange greetings at a distance.

Our next stop was four miles above Vicksburg, where the iron clad rounded up and blew her whistle, which was answered by that of a Confederate steamer coming for us. It was over three hours before she came in sight around the bend of the river, about a mile away. She was soon alongside and we were ordered to go on board of her. A heavy guard was placed along the side and every one was searched to see that he carried off nothing that was not his. Some of our boys who had been sick had saved up their bacon and had as much as fifteen or twenty pounds, and rather than give it back to the Yankees they threw it overboard. The transfer was soon made and the lines loosened and we, as happy a lot of men as ever lived, were on our way to the Confederate lines in Vicksburg, where we arrived after dark. Our instructions were to march to the depot about a half a mile away and I think that Captain McPherson and I, who got separated from the rest of the boys, walked the whole distance on molasses barrels. We were to get rations at the depot, and when we arrived there we found some of the boys getting theirs.

Captain McPherson and myself did not draw any rations, as we had saved up those which we had gotten from the Yankee steamer, but all the other boys and the wounded drew rations such as they were, consisting principally of

ACTUAL SERVICE – THE KENTUCKY CAMPAIGN

pones of cornbread and canteens of molasses. That was the largest pile of cornbread I ever saw in my life.

We went to the depot and got in the box cars ready to go to Jackson [Mississippi]. The conductor came around and wanted our transportation orders and we told him that we were just from Yankeedom and had none. He said that we would have to get off, and we said that we would not and got up considerable of a row, but when the other boys and the wounded began to come in, he changed his tune. We soon pulled out for Jackson, fifty-six miles distant, where we arrived at daylight. As soon as we landed Captain McPherson and myself made for a hotel to get something to eat, but failed and came back to the depot. By this time all the wounded had been unloaded and were lying around, but with no one paying any attention to them.

We bid them good-bye and took the train for Chattanooga. We had been told at Vicksburg that we would be regularly exchanged, but when we arrived at Chattanooga we found that it was mistake and we were sent to the parole camps. I have often wondered what became of the poor wounded we left at Jackson but I have never been able to learn. We were kept in the parole camps for some time and then given leave of absence to go home, and this was the only time I was at home during my four years of service.

This is the end of the story of the Kentucky campaign.

Chap. IV

The Mississippi Campaign

I wish to give an account of the Mississippi campaign when our division under General [John Cabell] Breckinridge was ordered to reinforce General [Joseph E.] Johnston, who was trying to get in [Ulysses S.] Grant's rear and help General [John C.] Pemberton out of Vicksburg, where he was besieged.

We took the train at Bridgeport, Tennessee, and went to Mobile [Alabama] and from there to Jackson, Mississippi, where we were ordered to draw three days' rations and put on the road leading to Black River. While we halted there some of the paroled prisoners from Pemberton's army came along and told us that Vicksburg had surrendered the day before [July 4, 1863]. We had to get pontoon bridges across the river, and, in order to do so, it was necessary to get a line across and volunteers were called for. The first one to step forward

Gen. Joseph E. Johnston

THE MISSISSIPPI CAMPAIGN

was Captain Simeon Strickland, then a beardless boy of eighteen or nineteen years, and he swam the river with the line and fastened it to the other side. He, nor anyone else, knew what danger there was ahead of him, but he did not stop on that account, but bravely did the duty for which he had volunteered.

When we heard that Vicksburg had surrendered we were put back on the road to Jackson, a distance of fifty miles. We marched all day, suffering terrible for water—after we left the rivers there was no water to be had except from mud holes. Our division was sent off on a settlement road to head off a Yankee regiment of cavalry which it was reported was trying to get around in our rear. The day was a terrible, hot day and we were sent on the double-quick for two or three miles. When we got to a stopping place we found that it was a false alarm and not more than a third of our men were left, the rest having fallen out from the intense heat. General Breckinridge himself came near fainting from the heat, and him on horseback.

We got back to Jackson that night at twelve o'clock and fell down under some old shelters and went to sleep. Before morning a terrible rain came up and the flood almost floated me out into the street. The next morning we threw our lines around the town and went to building breastworks behind which we were to receive Grant's army.

Chap. V

The Battle of Jackson, Mississippi

WE remained in our entrenchment for two days before Grant's army arrived. As soon as our breastworks were completed our brave Captain Saxon was sent out with the skirmish line. Sunday morning [July 7, 1863] at nine o'clock we commenced to hear the muskets fire from both sides and soon Captain Saxon was forced to fall back and join the main line behind the breastworks. As soon as our skirmish line had joined us behind the breastworks we could see the Yankee army in four lines of battle advancing on us.

Our forces had planted a battery of three cannons in our rear and opened a heavy fire over our heads into the advancing Grant's army, and every time a shell would plow through the Yankee lines it would leave an open street which they immediately closed up and continued to advance.

Our boys were anxious to repulse the advancing Yankee forces but the command was given, "Hold your fire, boys, hold your fire." And we did hold our fire until the Yankees were within eighty or ninety yards of our entrenchment, then we opened fire on them with telling effect, we made it so hot for them that they were thrown into complete confusion. They tried to re-form their lines and utterly failed in their

THE BATTLE OF JACKSON, MISSISSIPPI

efforts. During the skirmish two of the Yankee flag bearers ran up on our breastworks and we captured their flags.

Then we were ordered to jump the breastworks and follow the retreating Yankees. We followed them for a mile down the road.

As we went through the woods we came upon a Yankee soldier with one leg and one arm shot off but still alive and begging for water, but our canteens were empty and none of us had any to give him. It was hard indeed to see a man suffer so and not be able to relieve him with so much as a drink of water, but such is war.

The night we evacuated Jackson we fell back towards Pearl River, and when we came to the bridge we found that torpedoes had been placed in the road with guards to tell our men to bear to the right so as to miss them, and you may be sure that we kept well away in that direction. When we got a chance we dropped down and went to sleep, but were awakened by a terrible rattling. The men jumping up in their sleep hallooed that the Yankee cavalry was coming and three men ran over me and knocked me down and almost broke my arm, but the noise proved to be a team running away with an ambulance. The Grant army did not follow us any further than Brandon [Mississippi], and there we took the train for Chattanooga.

I can not close these reminiscences without a word of praise for Captain Saxon of our Company E, who was one of the best skirmish commanders in the Confederate Army. He was in command of our skirmish lines at Jackson and also at the bloody battle at Franklin, and in both places proved his bravery and capability, winning the highest praise from the commanding officers. Middle Florida sent no braver or more competent man to the front than Captain Saxon, and I hope that he is still alive and may read these lines so that he will know that some of those who were under him and saw him in action still remember him.

Chap. VI

The Battle of Missionary Ridge

I shall never forget the hard fight at Missionary Ridge [Chattanooga] nor the suffering of our men in the trenches before the battle for some three or four weeks. We had no tents and had to use our blankets stretched over poles to keep off the cold rains, and as few of our men had more than one blanket, their sufferings were intense. I have heard the men in Virginia complain of the cold there, but I am sure that it was no worse than that in front of Lookout Mountain. We were kept on the alert for three or four weeks before the fight came off, and you could hear the boys praying and wishing for the fight to come if it was coming, anything to get out of the suspense and suffering caused by lack of rations and shelter.

Our line stretched along the foot of Missionary Ridge and across the valley to the foot of Lookout Mountain, a distance of about twenty miles. Our picket line was in rifle pits about a hundred yards in advance of the main line and another hundred yards in advance of this was our vidette line in rifle pits also, but these could only be visited by night to bring relief on account of the proximity of the Yankee. Between them and our men a constant fire was kept up all day and even at night, and even the pickets had to keep low to be out of range. At night the only fire allowed was a few coals over which to warm their fingers and toes, for the slightest light would bring a musket ball in that direction, and the flashing of the muskets from both lines during the night made a grand sight if it were not for the fact that every flash meant a bullet, many of which found a billet in the body of some poor soldier.

The last night we were on the line it was very dark, and about three o'clock in the morning, while on vidette duty, I came near crawling into the Yankee lines, getting so close that I could hear a Yankee guard clear up his throat. I halted and got my bearings and crawled back to the pit I had just left. While warming my fingers over the few coals the men had in the pit, one asked if I did not hear the Yankees beating their coffee in their tin cups with their bayonets. One of our men by the name of Stockwell sung out to the Yankees and said, "You must be preparing an early breakfast?" To which the Yankees replied, "We are coming over to see us you Johnny Rebs today." That word "Johnny Reb" will never be forgotten by me.

I got back to my place in the line which was at the foot of Missionary Ridge, and just as day began to break [November 25, 1863] we could hear the Yankee officers giving the commands getting their men in line, though the underbrush was so thick that we could not see them. But soon after daylight they got a battery in position and began firing on us, though but little damage was done, as they were shooting too high. Soon we could see the heavy lines of battle of the Yankees advancing at a distance and it seemed as if the woods were alive with them, and we could see the officers dashing up and down their lines on their horses.

THE BATTLE OF MISSIONARY RIDGE

About this time our batteries in the rear of our line and further up the Ridge opened fire on them with shells, but it did not stop their advance, and shortly after, the musketry fire of our picket lines falling back could be heard, and there was heavy cannonading on both sides. About seven o'clock we could hear heavy firing on our right. By this time the Yankees were not more than two hundred yards in front of our lines, and we were ordered to open fire on them with musketry, which we did, making it so hot for them that after a while they retreated, but re-formed their lines and again advanced. We drove them back the third or fourth time, with dreadful loss every time, but they kept coming, and about three in the afternoon we got orders to fall back to the top of the Ridge. We had never given an inch and why we were ordered back I never knew unless the line on the right of us had given away. There had been heavy artillery fire all the time, but our big guns had been doing but little damage, shooting too high all the time. When we started up the Ridge the Yankees made it as hot for us as we had done for them before, and many of our men went down.

Our ammunition had been about exhausted when we were at the foot of the hill, but when we reached the top, sixty rounds additional were issued to the man, and when the Yankees charged us again we were ready and drove them back again and again. But the first thing we knew they came up behind cliffs and rocks and there was a hand-to-hand fight—Yankees and our men mixed up together. We were forced to retreat down the hill and it was there that our men were slaughtered, several of our boys being killed near me.

About this time General Bragg and his staff dashed by on their horses and one of them yelled to us, "Give them hell, boys," and just then one of them was shot from his large cream-colored horse, which ran off down our side of the hill. General Bragg was a brave old soldier even if he was a tyrant to his men. We had two flag bearers shot down and the third time General Bragg jumped from his horse and picked up the flag himself. Just as he mounted again, a lone soldier from the Third Florida ran up and took the flag from him and carried it safe to the rear.

When the Yankees broke our lines the order was given to retreat, but the men were retreating without orders, all of them that were not kept as prisoners by the Yankees, and there was a lot of them. As we ran down the hill, one of our boys, Eph Lassiter, cried to me, "Lieutenant, I am killed." At the bottom of the hill we halted for a moment and I looked at his wound and told him that he was not killed. A piece of shell had struck him on the shoulder and tore away a piece of flesh as large as a man's hand. He was losing blood very rapidly. I do not know whether he died or not, but I have never seen him since.

GEN. BRAXTON BRAGG

When we reached the bottom of the hill we came to the little bridge across the Chickamauga River, and there was a mix-up of men, artillery, ambulances and wagons, all trying to cross the river at once. The infantry was held back, though, and others allowed to go ahead.

THE BATTLE OF MISSIONARY RIDGE

We were ordered to fall in on a road leading down toward Dalton, Georgia. We had marched about half a mile when we came to a big pile of rations by the side of the road and were ordered to halt and fill our empty haversacks, which we were glad enough to do for we had fought all day with nothing to eat. Some got flour and some meal and some meat and some got no meat and some got syrup. My tent mate got a good piece of meat for himself and me. Some of the boys rolled out what they supposed to be a barrel of syrup and knocked the head in, when it proved to be a barrel of soft soap. Generally we were glad to get soap and have a wash day, but there was no time for this now. Of course, the rations were raw and we had no time to cook them as we were marched all night still hungry and tired—so tired that for my part I slept marching along. There was a large quantity of the rations left and some cavalry men told me that General Bragg had it burned, but he always did burn more rations than he gave his soldiers. The next morning we halted about sunrise, and our hungry men soon found the brigade wagon and got our cook pots and we cooked and ate once more.

While we lost the battle we had the satisfactory of knowing that we did not give an inch of ground except at the point of the bayonet and that the Yankees paid dearly in blood for every foot of ground they got from us. General Bragg was relieved soon afterward by General Joseph E. Johnston and we went in winter quarters near Dalton. I did not get much rest for I was sent down to Sugar Valley with a squad of about one hundred to build roads. The work was hard and regular but I had a good time all the same and so did most of the men. The young ladies there gave us a big Christmas dinner and dance.

SEVENTY-SEVEN YEARS IN DIXIE

I formed the acquaintance of two young ladies out in the country and one night wanted to go and see them and wanted to borrow the Captain's horse, but he was lame so I was given permission to ride an army mule. I left about dark and had gone but a short distance when I came to a ditch which I thought the mule would step over, but instead she jumped about ten feet and I landed on my head about ten feet ahead of her. I got up, brushed off the mud and remounted, and in due time arrived at the home of the young ladies where I had a very good time and might have had a better one if it had not been that there were two other soldiers there. About ten o'clock I left and started back. It was dark, so dark that I could not see the mule and soon found myself on the wrong road. The mule stopped and I could not see what the trouble was, but dug in my big cavalry spurs and when the mule brought up she was at the bottom of a railroad cut and it was early next morning when I got into camp.

Chap. VII

The Hundred Days Battle

THE great campaign of North Georgia, known as the One Hundred Days Battle, was fought by the Confederate Army of Tennessee under the command of the great and heroic General Joseph F. Johnston. They were confronted by the Federal army under command of General [William T.] Sherman, who had over 100,000 valiant soldiers.

After our army had remained in and around Dalton for several months in what was known as winter quarters, General Sherman began to advance from Chattanooga, and we were put on the march to meet his advance. I think our direction was north from Dalton, and it was but a few days before we could hear the fire at a distance of the heavy cannons.

The Federals were advancing rapidly and our work of fighting and throwing up breastworks soon commenced. If I remember right, our first fighting was at Rocky Face Mountain on May 12, 1864, and then for one hundred days it was a gradual retreat for the army of General Johnston. We would hold General Sherman's army in check all day, and as soon as night fell would evacuate our positions, fall back eight or ten miles, and then get the order to get our spades and dig rifle pits and pile logs for breastworks. By daylight we would be ready for the Yankees, and they rarely failed to come, either. Work all night and fight all day was our rule for the hundred days, but there was one good feature about it and that was that we had plenty of rations. General Johnston looked after the commissary much better than General Bragg.

At Resaca [Georgia – May 13-15, 1864] we had a severe battle and there we lost two of the brave boys from our company while crossing the bridge under a heavy fire of shell, grape and canisters. It was here that General Johnston came near getting his army in the nine hole, but his good generalship saved him, and he succeeded in getting his army safely across the bridge. He was too foxy for Sherman.

We had another hard fight at New Hope Church [Georgia] on May 25th and 26th, where our Florida brigade lost half its number in killed, wounded and taken prisoners. On the evening of the 28th our brigade was ordered to charge upon the Yankee works. The order was to jump our breastworks and charge the Yankee lines at the signal of a cannon fired on our left. About four o'clock the signal came, and the order "Attention" came from our Colonel D. A. McLean. Just as he sprang on the breastworks to give the command, a minié ball struck him squarely in the forehead and he dropped back in the trenches. The command was taken up by our major and over we went to the command, "Forward, guide center, quick time march!" I suppose we had gone about three hundred yards when we could see a lot of newly cut brush, and from behind it there rose the Yankees in three or four ranks. I know it seemed to me that the air was blue with their uniforms. As they rose they fired volley after volley into our single line of battle, and we returned the fire, but soon had

THE HUNDRED DAYS BATTLE

to fall back, leaving over half our men killed, wounded or prisoners of the field. Many of our best men were lost there and are now sleeping there under the oaks of North Georgia.

The charge and the loss of our men there was useless, for the order had been countermanded, but the courier by whom the order was sent failed to reach us in time to stop the charge. We buried our dead that night after dark and a sad job it was. I helped to bury one of my closest friends, Lieutenant Cobb of Company D. He was hit near the shoulder in the back as we were retreating towards the works.

There was an old widow lady living in the rear of our breastworks who had a fine lot of bacon, which she asked us to bury to keep the Yankees from getting it. We dug a hole about the size of a grave and put the meat in it with some boards on top of it and then filled in the dirt, placing a head and foot board up to make it look more like a grave.

That night we slipped out and marched ten or twelve miles toward Atlanta, and then began again the work of building breastworks without any rest or sleep.

Thus it went, fight and fall back and throw up breastworks until near Atlanta, when the war department made the sad change from General Johnston to General [John B.] Hood. All the officers and men loved

GEN. JOHN BELL HOOD

Johnston and none of us believed that had he been kept in command that Sherman would have made his famous raid through Georgia. But as soon as Hood was placed in command he put us to fighting one against five in the open field.

Our first fighting experience under him was the charge we made in the evening at Peach Tree Creek [July 20, 1864] near Atlanta. We kept up this fighting until Sherman got a part of his army around in our rear when we had to fall back from Atlanta to Jonesboro [Georgia]. I well remember the night we left Atlanta and marched all night in heavy marching order, reaching Jonesboro eighteen miles distant just at daylight, and met Sherman's soldiers there at the railroad and went to fighting for its possession. Our division soon got orders to fall back and build breastworks of fence rails, but when the Yankees turned their artillery loose at us the flying rails killed and wounded more than the shells from the Yankees. None of the officers had the faith in Hood that they had in Johnston and none believed that the change should have been made.

I was on duty during the whole hundred days and never lost a day during the whole time.

Chap. VIII

The Battle of July 22nd

During the siege of Atlanta Generals Pat Cleburne's and Frank Cheatham's corps were sent around to attack Sherman's extreme right. We marched through the streets of Atlanta about dark on the night of the 21st of July [1864] and kept going all that night, marching twenty miles without a minute for rest or sleep. About daylight we were halted and the command was given, "In place, rest." We fell down on the ground, every man with his gun in his hand, and soon fell asleep. I presume we were there about an hour when we

Gen. Patrick Ronayne Cleburne

Gen. Benjamin Franklin Cheatham

were awakened by the command "Attention" and formed in line of battle. Some of the field officers were dashing up and down in front in the lines and the boys, though tired and sleepy, were in good spirits and laughed about going into it so early.

When we moved in line of battle we left the road we had come on from Atlanta and marched through the woods. After about a quarter of a mile we came to a rail fence and the order was to go over it and keep our lines intact. We did the best we could, and, after halting a moment to straighten them, we went on, the orders being given in low tone and with directions to the men not to speak above a whisper. We went through a large field of corn and out on the other side over another rail fence and into the thick woods, still keeping a good line, however. About 150 yards further on we came to a ravine about as wide as we could jump and over that we went, and then the command was passed to double-quick, and as we got to the top of a little hill we went into the Yankees' camp. Some of them were just getting out of bed and we fired a couple of volleys and then they surrendered, some of them in their night clothes. We captured all their tents, guns and wagons, but they were soon reinforced and we were compelled to retreat, but got back to Atlanta with about two hundred prisoners.

A Georgia brigade under General Jackson was on our right, and in crossing the ravine they got mixed up and the General was riding up and down the line hallooing, "Good Lord, where is my brigade?" If it had not been for this we would have made our surprise more complete. Captain Slocumb got his two brass pieces in position down this ravine but was too late to do us any good, and in attempting

THE BATTLE OF JULY 22ND

to get out, one of his ammunition wagons jammed between two trees and a detail from the First Florida was ordered to help him out, and I was in this detail. The Yankees had a battery in position by this time and were pouring in grape and canister on us and killing horses and men.

We finally got the cannon out all right, but lost four horses and four men by the explosion of a cannon caisson which was set on fire by a shell from the Yankee artillery. It was a hot place about that time, I tell you. It was the 22nd of July and hot as it gets to be, and we made for a shade near a log house which the people had left to get out of the range of the firing. While resting there John Wheeler and Stockwell got a window of the house open and found a big churn of buttermilk and brought it out under the shade to us, and I do not think that milk ever tasted so good to me as that did.

In fighting there the Yankees lost one of their best men, General McPherson.

Chap. IX

The Battle of Franklin, Tennessee – The Worst Battle of the War

When General Hood was trying to get in General Sherman's rear north of Atlanta, our first place to strike the railroad leading from Atlanta to Nashville was at Dalton, which at that time was guarded by a regiment of Negroes commanded by white officers, who, by the way, were all mounted on white horses. We arrived in front of the place early in the morning and our General [William B.] Bate sent in a flag of truce to demand its surrender, which was granted without firing a shot, and the troops were turned over to our brigade to guard. It seems that up to this time the soldiers had all been barefooted, but when they found they had to surrender, new shoes were issued to the entire regiment and when they marched into our lines every man of them had new footwear. Our commander saw what had been done, and under his direction we exchanged shoes with the prisoners, and the next morning our men all had new shoes and they were barefoot again. We guarded them for three days, but what became of them afterwards I never knew. The only trouble about the shoes was that they were all number elevens and were too big for us, but we wore them just the same.

THE BATTLE OF FRANKLIN, TENNESSEE

About three miles from Dalton the Yankees had a block house built of hewn oak logs, and when our commander sent a flag of truce to demand its surrender the Yankees refused to recognize it and fired on the two officers carrying it, one of them, Captain Miney, having his horse shot under him. They came back to the command and General Bate ordered his two brass thirty-two-pounders turned loose at the house, and every time they fired, the splinters flew. After a few rounds another flag of truce was sent in and this time they surrendered, about eighty of them. The block house was fitted with small loopholes from which they fired, killing and wounding a number of our men. The next morning my messmate and myself went in the house, which was quite dark inside, to see if we could find anything to eat. I was feeling around on the ground and found something cold that felt like a piece of meat, and when I picked it up and took it to the light, I found it to be an ear that had been shot off of one of the soldiers who had been in there. It was a big flat ear but I had no appetite.

From there we marched to Columbia [Tennessee – November 24, 1864] on the Duck River, at which place the Yankees were stationed. General Cheatham was in command and next morning a detail of one hundred men was ordered and marched down the river about three miles. A staff officer put me in command with instruction to build a bridge over which the infantry could cross. His instructions were to build trusses with legs ten feet long, put stringers on these and floor the bridge with rails. We went to work and by night had the trusses ready but the pontoon train which was to put them up in the river had not shown up and it was reported that it had been captured. We kept at work as best we could and about one o'clock at night the pontoon train came and went to work setting up the trusses. On the opposite bank was a high bluff and about half my men were taken over and put to work making a cut through that and worked all night without flinching, but the next morning when General Pat Cleburne arrived with his brigade ready to cross, the cut was not finished.

General Cleburne called for the officer in charge and I reported, politely saluting him as he sat there on his big blaze-faced sorrel horse. He wanted to know why the work had not been completed and I told him that I did all possible with the men that I had, that not a man had closed his eyes all night. He was mad about it and abused me shamefully, and threatened to have me arrested and court-martialed for my failure, but I was never arrested. He sent a lot of his men over to the other side and put them to work on the cut and soon had it finished and got his men over along with a few ambulances. General Cheatham soon followed him with his corps, but neither had any artillery or wagons except a few ambulances. The working detail was ordered to get their guns and fall in with their commands and we started to Spring Hill [Tennessee – November 29, 1864], said to be about nineteen miles distant, which we reached about four in the afternoon, but still no sleep. General [Robert E.] Lee's corps was in front of Columbia to hold the Yankees in check until we got around in the rear.

When we arrived in Spring Hill we were thrown in line of battle and ordered to advance against the Yankees, and we soon drove them back to the railroad. When dark came and we were ordered to cease firing, we lay down to sleep in line of battle so near the road that we could hear the Yankee

THE BATTLE OF FRANKLIN, TENNESSEE

officers giving the commands to their men as they marched along. Some of the officers said afterward that if General Hood had not been drunk the charge would not have been stopped. The Yankees who had slipped by General Lee in the night and gone to Franklin would have been cut off if our advance had gone a dozen yards further, as we would have been in possession of the railroad, which General [Nathan Bedford] Forrest with his gallant cavalry had struck the day before and blockaded with several overturned cars.

GEN. ROBERT E. LEE

In the evening the Yankees had several heavy guns playing on us and a number of our men were killed and wounded. During the charge I stepped over a man who had been struck with a cannon ball that had cut off half of his head. I have often wondered who he was and what regiment he belonged to.

The next morning [November 30, 1864] before sunrise we were put on the road to Franklin, said to be about nineteen miles, and this was another forced march. All that day we passed Yankee wagons on the road that had been captured by General Forrest's men, the mules shot or taken and the wagons plundered and left standing in the road. Often when our advance guard would reach the top of a hill they could see the Yankee rear-guard some two or three miles in advance. About four o'clock we arrived within about three miles of Franklin and were thrown in line of battle, and our division commander, General [John Calvin] Brown, came down the line and made us a little talk. He said that the Yankees had thrown up breastworks, but they were temporary and we could go right over them, and with this done we would go right on to Nashville and asked us if we would follow him. We gave the rebel yell and said that we would follow him.

Our skirmish line, in command of Captain Saxon, was thrown out and soon drove the Yankee pickets in, and then the main line was ordered forward.

The skirmish line under Captain Saxon drove the Yankees out of their first line of breastworks, but was compelled to retire to the main line, and the muskets began popping in all directions, coming and going hot from both sides until our lines drove them out of their second line of works. When they fell back to their main line our boys began dropping like corn before a hail storm, and we never did succeed in reaching their main line, for about fifty yards in front of it they had cut down a lot of thorny locust bushes and it was impossible in face of the hot fire to get through them.

When it was seen that we could not get through this brush line the order was given to lie down. It was the only hope for us, for we could neither go forward or go back in such a fire and live. This was about seven o'clock in the evening and we laid there under that terrific fire until about eleven when all at once the firing ceased, and then and not until then could we do anything to relieve the sufferings of the wounded, who were all around us and begging for water. Their piteous cries ring in my ears to this day and I often

THE BATTLE OF FRANKLIN, TENNESSEE

dream of them. When it was learned that the enemy had slipped out of their breastworks and gone, our thin lines arose but it was thin indeed, for over two-thirds of our men had dropped.

No commands were given that I heard of, and it seemed to be every man for himself. Myself and Lieutenant James Hart got together and began looking for water and something to eat. He had lost his haversack during the fighting in the evening and I had nothing but a piece of cold cornbread in my old dirty haversack, but we ate that without any water, and afterward decided to go down into the town in the search for water and something more to eat. We worked our way through the brush and over the breastworks and as we got down on the inside we stumbled over the dead bodies of the killed there.

It was about half a mile from there down to the business part of town and when we arrived there everything was shut up. Not a ray of light from any residence or business house and we went to four or five houses before we found anyone. At last we got an answer and a long, thin, middle-aged, smooth-shaven man came to the door and asked us what we wanted and who we were. We told him that we were Confederate soldiers from the battlefield and wanted water and something to eat. He asked us where the Yankees were and we told him that they had all gone on the road to Nashville. He then took us through the house into another room where there were three or four ladies and some men, and they were a badly frightened lot, but seemed somewhat relieved when we told them that the Yankees had gone. They gave us water and the ladies soon had us a good supper fixed up for which we were hungry enough to do full justice.

SEVENTY-SEVEN YEARS IN DIXIE

About that time all the cannons, that General Hood had said to be about three hundred pieces, came up and were put in position near the bridge which the Yankees had just crossed, and commenced firing. It was the most terrific cannonading that I ever heard and made the dishes from which we were eating fairly rattle on the table and nearly frightened the men and women into fits.

Some of our boys who were first out on the road toward Nashville next morning told me that they saw dead Yankees five and six miles out on the road that had been killed by that cannonading that night. In all my four years' service I never heard such a roar as they made that night.

We soon finished our supper or breakfast, for it was past midnight and daylight soon came, and we started back to the battlefield. We asked the men there to go back with us and two of the young men started and went as far as the breastworks, but when they saw the dead men there their hearts failed them and they turned back.

When my comrade and I reached the breastworks we met an officer who told me that I was to go to the Carter house and join the burial detail. When I got there I was placed in charge of about fifty men and the next two days was the most horrible that I ever put in, in my life. Though it has been more than forty years since then, the scenes of that battlefield are as fresh in my mind as though it was yesterday. I think the hardest fighting must have been near the old gin house on Pike Road, for there the bodies were so thick that we could have stepped from one to another, and to think that these were our own boys, who had left all that was near and dear to them to fight for the cause they believed was right.

THE BATTLE OF FRANKLIN, TENNESSEE

THE CARTER HOUSE
The bullet-ridden walls can still be seen today
at this historic site in Franklin, Tennessee.

One of the first things I saw that morning was General Pat Cleburne's old sorrel horse astraddle of the Yankee breastworks, just as he had tried to jump over. We went up to him and lying just over inside the breastworks was the body of the General and near his that of General [John] Adams, both surrounded by the bodies of the Yankee and Confederate dead.

About this time a general rode up and, calling us to attention, made a flowery speech praising the fighting we had done and said that no printed history would ever record braver men than we had proven ourselves during the terrific fighting of the night before. The tears rolled down his cheeks as he talked, and he turned and rode off. I did not know who he was, and while some of the boys said that they thought that he was a Mississippi general, I have always thought that it was General [Edward C.] Walthall, who did such good fighting on the pike road before Nashville just before our lines were broken by the Yankees getting in behind us.

After completing our work as the burial detail we were ordered to rejoin our commands and we were soon on the road to Murphreesboro. General Bate's division of infantry and General Forrest's division of cavalry were in command. I do not remember the distance, but I do remember that we got there in time to get a good licking [December 5-7, 1864]. We got there about noon and were formed in line of battle, the cavalry being dismounted and put on our right. We had been told that there were only about three hundred Yankees there but there were nearer ten thousand and they ran right over us. We fired a few volleys but had to give way. In the advance we went through the old cemetery where our boys were buried that had fallen in the first fight there about two years before.

GEN. NATHAN BEDFORD FORREST

As we fell back through the cedar grove I noticed a number of places where the bones of those buried there in

THE BATTLE OF FRANKLIN, TENNESSEE

the fight before were sticking up through the ground and it seemed as if they must have been buried very shallow and more rubbish than dirt thrown in the graves.

After we had fallen back and re-formed our lines Generals Forrest and Bate had a big row about some parts of the line giving way too soon, and I thought they would shoot one another, but some other officers got between them and stopped the row.

We took up the march from here to the railroad leading from Murphreesboro to Nashville, striking it about ten miles north of the former place, capturing two block houses on the road to Nashville. We stopped about dark and sat up all night burning rails to keep from freezing, so cold was the weather. The next day we rejoined the remainder of the army and went to digging ditches.

Chap. X

The Battle of Nashville, Tennessee

AFTER our hard and bloody fight at Franklin, we advanced twenty miles toward Nashville, where we remained nine days in throwing up breastwork and building what was called redoubts. The weather was very cold—we worked both night and day getting our fortifications ready for the fight on the morning of the ninth [of December 1864]. The enemy advanced on us from Nashville, which was four miles distance, and about ten o'clock in the day the Yankees drove our picket line and the fight became general all along the lines. General Walthall's brigade was in line of battle on the pike road leading from Franklin to Nashville, at which place was the hardest fighting done.

We were on a little hill to the left of General Walthall's brigade, which could be seen plainly from our hill, and the first shots were

Gen. Edward Cary Walthall

THE BATTLE OF NASHVILLE, TENNESSEE

made on the pike road by lines of battle by Negro troops; the Negroes made some four or five different charges on Walthall's brigade and were repulsed in every charge, leaving the field black with dead. There was one charge made by the Negro troops that I noticed in particular. Walthall's men never fired a gun until the Negroes got up within about seventy or eighty yards of their breastworks, then they opened the deadly fire with our boys' bullets almost demolishing the Negro ranks to the ground. I think that it was the last charge they made on General Walthall's brigade—that was the best fighting done that day. Walthall's troops repulsed them five different times. When the Negroes failed to break Walthall's lines, they moved further to our left and broke our lines.

About the time our lines were broken a flanking party had been sent around in our rear, and it was a general fallback by Hood's whole army—a general stampede. We fell back across the pike road; down that road was blue with Yankees, and they were closing in on us and pouring heavy volleys into us. It appeared to me that the air was filled with shells and bullets. A perfect stampede had taken place among the whole army—Yankees and our men all mixed together; some surrendering, some falling dead, others trying to get up the hill to make their escape, the colonels and generals dashing across the hills trying to rally the men with pistols and swords drawn over their retreating men. The generals would get thirty or forty men rallied in a squad and dash off to rally another squad, when the first rallied would break ranks and run for life. Our wagons and ambulances were left with the Yankees to be captured. Myself and messmate ran by where a soldier was trying to cut his mules loose from his wagon. He said to us, "Boys, for God's sake, help me get my mules loose from the wagon!"

I said in reply, "Let your damned mules go and try to save yourself."

The Yankees had our guns turned on us. Myself and partner made the top of the hill. As we were running a big shell busted just above our heads, passing so near our heads until the force of it knocked us both to our knees and struck a man just a few steps from us. It must have knocked him ten feet up in the air. When we arrived at the top of the mountain we stopped a moment and looked back down in the valley where our wagons, men and Yankees were all mixed up together. It was a bad sight to see our men waving their white handkerchiefs flying, surrendering to the Yankees.

We must have lost one-half of our wagon train which was left down in that valley. Myself and partner at last got into the road leading to Franklin along with a lot more of our men. It was said to be nineteen miles to Franklin. The wagon train that escaped was ahead of us on the road to Franklin. It cut the red clay up and made it about half-leg deep in mud, and it was very dark and sometimes we would have to stop and pull men out of the mud. We were marching under no orders whatever—every man for himself. A great many of our men completely gave out and some of them would crawl up into the hind-part of the wagons. I thought several times that I would have to fall out for I was completely broken down, but when I would think of being captured I would come to a new life. About the break of day next morning we arrived back into Franklin; about one dozen of us fell down under some old sheds and fell asleep, and about nine o'clock

THE BATTLE OF NASHVILLE, TENNESSEE

we were waked by some commanding officer. We were then ordered to look up our regiment and when we all got together, about one-half of the regiment were missing. We then marched for Tennessee River where we were to put our pontoon bridge in to cross the army on, when the Yankees sent five gunboats to meet us there to prevent us from putting our bridge across the river. But our intoxicated commander put all the sharpshooters we had left, with their long-range one-thousand-yard guns, along the bank of the river and whipped the gunboats back down the river; then we put our brigade across the river over into Alabama and then marched for Corinth, Mississippi, where we were put under command of General Dick Taylor.

Chap. XI

Our Last Battle in the War

A FTER our retreat from Nashville, we went to Corinth where we stayed four or five days. We had captured six so-called bushwhackers. We were marched out to an old field the fifth morning and drawn up in line; those six bushwhackers were placed down upon their knees fastened with their hands tied behind them to a stake. Twelve men with loaded guns were marched in front of the six men, and orders were given by the officers in command of the twelve men to fire, and the six men dropped dead except one, who was shot the second time. Our whole command was marched along by the six dead bodies.

A little incident that shows what men will do sometimes, occurred when our ragged remnant of Hood's army was going to reinforce Johnston in South Carolina. After moving down through the Mississippi Valley onto the Alabama River, we took the steamboat for Montgomery [Alabama]. We took the train to Columbus, Georgia, and when we reached there we were formed in line in the street while the ladies of the town gave us a splendid supper from baskets. We took the train again for Macon [Georgia], the higher officers all being in the rear coach, and some of the boys, to have a good time in Macon, pulled the coupling pin and dropped off this rear

OUR LAST BATTLE IN THE WAR

coach, so when we got to Macon we had no generals. They were good and mad but could never find out who it was that pulled the coupling pin.

From Macon we went to Milledgeville [Georgia] where we took up a line of march through the country to Augusta [Georgia]. Here we crossed a very large bridge over into South Carolina, then onto Chesterfield near where we got into North Carolina. We marched direct through the state until we met Sherman's army at Bentonville [March 19-21, 1865], then we whipped Sherman's troops and drove them back and also captured a lot of the Yankees' baggage and guns. This battle was the last battle of war with us.

We were then commanded by General J. E. Johnston. Soon after our fight at Bentonville, we fell back to the railroad leading from Greensboro to Wilmington [North Carolina] and went to camps at a station called Smithfield, where we remained six or seven days. Then we received orders to go up to the commissary and draw four days' rations, blue beef and musty corn meal—every soldier to cook up his four days' rations and be ready to march at four o'clock next morning. We were all ready to march on the road at the appointed time—we were put on what our generals called a forced march for four days and nights and ate our blue beef and musty, half-cooked cornbread as we marched along the long road. The word was that we were trying to meet General Lee's army; it seems to me that we crossed a great many creeks and other streams of water on that four days' long march through North Carolina. Some of the creeks were so deep that our men had to put their equipment on top of their heads. We waded every stream we came to, the water would take us up to the armpits—the order was to hurry up to meet Lee. The night of the fourth day's march we were up near Greensboro, where we halted about nine o'clock and were ordered to stack arms and rest. By the time I stopped and sat down I was asleep and knew nothing more until the next morning.

I was awakened by the voice of some commanding officer calling the soldiers to attention. He said that the order was for all the soldiers to remain in place until further orders. Some of the boys yelled to the officer to bring rations around, that they had not eaten anything in two days—it is true to say that there was a great many men who would eat up four days' rations in two days. I believe that most of our command was out of rations after about two days and nothing else to eat. About eight o'clock the same morning General Brown, our division commander, came around on our part of the lines and called the command to attention and said:

> *My fellow soldiers, I have sad news to tell you. We have struck arms here for the purpose to surrender to General Sherman. General Johnston is now in conference with General Sherman coming to the terms of surrendering [April 18, 1865]. General*

OUR LAST BATTLE IN THE WAR

Lee has surrendered already. I advise you, good soldiers, to remain as you are and get your parole and try to get back to your old homes. Our army is completely surrounded by the enemy.

Then General Brown turned his large, black horse around to bid us farewell; a regular yell turned loose along the lines saying, "General Brown, we want rations. We are hungry and must have something to eat!" This was the fifth day since we drew the four days' rations.

General Brown turned and fronted the lines again and says, "Boys, our side has no more rations for you. I will see that you get rations from the other side."

Some of the men says, "General, we want something to eat today."

The General turned again in riding off. He says, "Good soldiers, I will get you something just as soon as I possibly can." I believe if I remember right we got no rations for three or four days after General Brown had left us. I believe it was the night of the third day when the rations came to our part of the lines, but when it did come, it came plentifully, good bacon, hard biscuits, sugar and good coffee. There was heavy eating done for a while—the Yankees were very kind to us, but now and then there would be one that would throw off on us. Myself and several others went up on the hill in the old field where all our wagons, cannons, ambulances, horses and mules were parked for the Yankees. There I got a very large mare, one of the battery horses that helped to pull our cannons. I got one old saddle and bridle and rode this mare home to Florida. I was three weeks in the saddle—I came through North Carolina, South Carolina, Georgia, Alabama and into the Sea Coast of Florida. My old mare brought me through all of that long distance, but before I got halfway to Florida my old mare was as blind as a bat, and she died at my old home.

Coming through Georgia it was a very hard matter to get anything to eat or to get feed for my horse. I was very hungry one day about noon and noticed a good-looking house a short distance from the roadside. I thought that I would try to get dinner and my horse fed. I had tried several houses back on the road for something to eat but failed and I had not had breakfast, so I rode up to this house and hallooed.

OUR LAST BATTLE IN THE WAR

The landlady came out on the porch. Soldier-like I asked for something to eat and feed for my horse. In those days soldiers never called at a house for a meal, for if he did, he failed to get it. This good lady answered my call, "Who are you? A Yankee?"

I readily answered, "I am a Confederate soldier going home."

The good lady said, "Alight and bring your horse inside." I was very soon inside and met the landlady on the porch. She said, "We have but little for ourselves, but we will divide with a Confederate soldier. The mean old Yankees came along here the other day and took everything we had."

I told the good lady that the war was over and the soldiers are going home and she said, "Good news, daughter, and let us fix this soldier a good dinner, the war is over. I am so glad your papa will be home soon." She sure did give me a good dinner. After I finished eating I asked the lady what I owed for dinner and feeding my horse. She answered, "Nothing," but I paid her twenty-five dollars in Confederate money.

I said to the lady, "I have not told you the bad part of the war. Lee's and Johnston's armies are both surrendered, and we are whipped in the hands of the Yankees." The good woman almost shed tears.

I believe I was three weeks getting to Geneva, Alabama, near the line of Florida.

Chap. XII

The Little Wonder That Never Was Satisfied

This story tells of two little baby girls who were very hungry. Late in the evening when General Lee was falling back slowly before the enemy in front of Richmond, Virginia, he saw that it was important to plan a battle to save Richmond. He was forming his lines of battle through the thick underbrush to meet the great army of the North.

He saw it was necessary to have all the families that would be in danger of shells and shot to move to the rear, out of danger. The mother of these two little girls was near General Lee's lines, and General Lee sent his headquarters' wagons to the aid of this noble family to move them to the rear at once.

When the wagons arrived they were soon loaded and off for the rear with those little baby girls and furniture. After traveling all night they found themselves near a neighbor's house and they stopped for a call and a few minutes' rest. Daylight was just approaching and those two little girls had been hurried off from their home that night without supper and they were very hungry. This lady neighbor called the refugees in to have breakfast, so the retreating lady with her two hungry little girls were soon out of the wagon and in the house around the cook stove waiting for the biscuits to get

THE LITTLE WONDER THAT NEVER WAS SATISFIED

done. But it seemed that the woman's stove was filled with green wood and those little girls were waiting and watching those biscuits to get done, but it was all in vain. A staff officer came up and said those wagons must go to the rear at once, so the little girls were forced away and did not see the biscuits done.

Several years afterwards, when those little girls were young ladies, one of them wrote a little piece about the biscuits. Her little wonder was this: "Did those biscuits ever get done?"

Chap. XIII

Summary

These Battles of '61 – '65
Were Fought by the Boys in Gray

COMRADES of Fishing Creek, Shiloh, Perryville, Murfreesboro, Jackson, Chickamauga, Missionary Ridge, Kennesaw Mountain, Peach Tree Creek, Atlanta, the battle of the 22nd of July near Atlanta, Jonesboro, Franklin, Nashville, Bentonville, our last battle on this historic battlefield, amid the roar of cannons, shrieks of shells, the rattle of musketry, and the shouts of living and groans of the wounded and dying, cheering each other on to victory or defeat, or death ties of affectionate friendships were formed that bind us into one brotherhood by an invisible chain that is being shortened link by link, and ere long the last link will be broken in the presence of the new-made grave, some of the tenderest recollections of our lives are awakened and brought forth from memory, memories however sad, dear alike to you and me, because they are embalmed in sorrow, suffering, sacrifice and tears.

The visitation of this sad dispensation of an all-wise and a most merciful God, visibly reminds each of us old

SUMMARY

comrades that at best, a very few years remain to us upon this earth.

Let us this day resolve to make our callings and election sure and so live that when the roll is called up yonder we will have an unbroken reunion of all Confederate veterans who risked their all amid privation and suffering for four long years in defense of all that is dearest to man, home and loved ones, and to protect and maintain the most brilliant and magnificent civilization the world has ever known—that of our Southland. Every Confederate soldier's tombstone is as touching as his last tear upon the white bosom of his young manhood's bride and as tender as his farewell words to those who will sit among the graves of the Confederate veterans some future day and write sweeter songs than mortal ears ever heard before, because each tombstone is a volume within itself.

Forty-five years ago the 26th day of April, 1865, the Confederate flag, with its cross of its stars and bars, was furled at Greensboro, North Carolina, for the last time, and we are content to let it stay so forever. There is enough of glory and sacrifice encircled in its folds, not only to enshrine it in our hearts forever, but the trumpet of fame that must be silenced within it ceases to proclaim the splendid achievement over which that flag floated while we wore the gray four long years.

I am sincerely Seventy-Seven Years in Dixie.

H. W. REDDICK
SANTA ROSA, FLORIDA

Chap. XIV

Civil War Poems

CIVIL WAR POEMS

THE GOOD OLD CONFEDS

The good old Confeds marched over hills, fields, and valleys,
On lots of battlefields they discharged many roaring volleys.
They knew not what moment that would be their last,
That they would be slaughtered in the fields of the blast.
They marched over broad fields from East to the West,
To fight for their rights which they thought best.
The good old Confeds in Gray,
Are now at home in peace,
We hope each one a long, happy life,
And at home he may stay.
Let us now do honors to the "Good old Confeds,"
For it won't be long before
They'll all be dead.
We must not forget our Mothers
Who stayed and kept their homes,
Praying, and working at their looms.
The war is now ended between the North and South,
'Twas four long years spent at the cannon's mouth.
My Father allowed me this space in his little book,
Which is an opportunity I gladly took.

WALKER H. REDDICK
NOMA, FLORIDA

SEVENTY-SEVEN YEARS IN DIXIE

THE BOYS IN GRAY OF '61 – '65

Who fears to speak of "Sixty One"
    Who blushes at its fame?
When cowards sneer at deeds then done,
    Who hangs his head in shame?

He's all a knave or half, a slave,
    Who slights his record thus:
But a true man like you men,
    Will fill his glass with us.

We drink the memory of the brave,
    The faithful not a few,
Some lie near Potomac's wave,
    Some sleep in "Oakdale too."

Hundreds are gone, but still live on,
    The names of those who died,
All true men like you men,
    Remember them with pride.

Some 'neath the sods of distant States,
    Their patient hearts have laid,
Where with the stranger's heedless haste,
    Their unwatched graves were made.

But though their clay be far from us,
    Where friends may never come,
In true men like you men,
    Their spirit's still at home.

CIVIL WAR POEMS

The dust of some is Southern earth:
    Among their own they rest,
For the same land that gave them birth
    Has caught them to her breast.

And we will pray that from their clay
    Full many a race may start,
Of true men like you men,
    To act as brave a part.

They rose in dark and evil days,
    To right their native land:
They kindled here a living blaze,
    That nothing could withstand.

Alas, that might should vanquish right!
    They fell, and passed away.
And true men like you men,
    Are far too few today.

Then here's their mem'ry, may it be
    For us a guiding light,
To cheer, though lost our liberty,
    And lead us in the right!

Thru good and ill be patriots still,
    By each good impulse stirred.
And you men, be true men,
    Like the dead of the gallant Third.

(AUTHOR UNKNOWN)
SELECTED BY JOHN H. REDDICK
SANTA ROSA, FLORIDA

SEVENTY-SEVEN YEARS IN DIXIE

BENEFITS OF THE CIVIL WAR

The war, known as the Civil War,
Which the men in Gray fought so noble to win,
Was not without benefits to us,
And even now we can see them.

It was inevitable, it could no more
Have been avoided than you could have stayed
The movements of the tides.

The world will be the final arbiter,
So long as society remains irrational, and human
Governments are imperfect;
But the war, with all its dark catalogue of horrors,
Brought many many blessings.

It developed the many virtues of our people,
And taught them to be more self-sacrificing.

Again, the war built upon more certain and enduring foundations the government of the United States, and it firmly stands upon a broader and stronger basis than before.

The question may be asked, "Were we honest in our convictions and sincere in our alignage to the Confederate States?" We may most assuredly say, "Yes," nor does this affect our loyalty to the government of the United States.

It is something to have illustrated the valor of a people, to have carried a nation's flag without dishonor through a hundred battles and set an example to coming eyes of what unselfish heroism can accomplish.

CIVIL WAR POEMS

And the day is not far distant when the courage and heroic deeds of these brave and noble men will be recognized as the common heritage and glory of a prosperous and patriotic people.

All honor is due this dear old soldier who has composed this little book as a token of the brave and heroic deeds of his countrymen and himself, who is hale and hearty at the age of SEVENTY-SEVEN, and may he survive many happy years on earth with us yet.

ETTIE LOUISE STRICKLAND
INDA, MISSISSIPPI

CIVIL WAR POEMS

All Soon Be Gone

In eighteen hundred and sixty-one
The war between the States had just begun.
There came a call for manly men–
Both father and son enlisted then.
They were true, brave and strong;
Only a few more years and they'll all be gone.

We meet them everywhere we go,
Some are lame, halt, and blind, you know.
God knows we love them. He loves them more.
It was for a noble cause, and Oh!
When the guns begin to roar,
Brave, true and noble men onward they would go.

And then we thought they'd come back to stay,
Let's honor them while they live, they'll soon go away,
But don't forget their loved ones were at home,
They worked, tugged, wove and spun,
Prayers were heard from every loom,
    "God save our noble men!"

Confederate soldiers they were brave and true,
    As they marched under the RED WHITE AND BLUE.
        Say kind words to them as you go on
            For they all will soon be gone.

Arthur B. Harrison
Noma, Florida

SEVENTY-SEVEN YEARS IN DIXIE

The Blue and the Gray

In battle array the Blue and the Gray,
    Met in arms on the soils of the South,
        And without any fear, though life was so dear,
To be spent at the cannon's mouth.

Fierce was the fight for what was deemed right,
    By the warriors, each for his own,
        But little the care each other would share
If the future could only atone.

Then came the glad day for the Blue and the Gray
    To depart from the fields of the strife:
        Once more to engage (And peace was the wage)
In the goodlier callings of life.

Oh! Great was the blight, whether wrong or right,
    Of the war of the Blue and the Gray,
        And sad was the song, howe'r grievous the wrong,
In the hearts of the people that day.

So many were lost of that mighty host
    That marched to the beat of the drum,
        That their graves are found on every mound–
They never would homeward come.

But there's never a wrong that hasn't its song
    Of a right and a triumph, too;
        And the triumph is sung, by every tongue,
Of the war of the Gray and the Blue.

CIVIL WAR POEMS

For in freedom's own land united we stand
    On the ashes of hate and strife;
        And as peace will endure so our flag is secure
As the emblem of National life.

All honor today for the Blue and the Gray
    Whether they fought for the right or the wrong;
        Their old story is told and 'twill never grow old–
'Tis a glorious triumph song.

                            (AUTHOR UNKNOWN)
                        SELECTED BY VELMA MCDONALD
                              SANTA ROSA, FLORIDA

SEVENTY-SEVEN YEARS IN DIXIE

The Gray and the Blue

Two armies covered hill and plain
    Each fought with all might and main,
General Scott pressed forward that day
    With his boys in blue,
        While Beauregard said to his boys in gray:
        "To the flag we'll stand true."

The soldiers flocked down to the banks,
    Till bordered by its pebbles.
        One wooded shore was blue with "Yanks,"
        And one was gray with "Rebels."

When all was silent, and the band,
    With movement bright and tricksy,
        Made forest and stream, hill and strand,
        Reverberate with "Dixie"

Then a pause and then again,
    The boisterous trumpets pealed
        And "Yankee Doodle" was the strain,
        And the music was revealed.

In Blue or Gray the soldier sees
    As by a wand of a fairy,
        The cottage 'neath the live-oak trees,
        The cabin by the prairie.

                          IDA DAVIS
                         MERIDIAN, MISSISSIPPI

CIVIL WAR POEMS

The Parting Volley

With arms reversed the ranks passed on,
   The muffled drum marks flattered tread,
     A muster roll reads simply gone,
         One more is numbered with the dead.
            A Crash! The parting volley rolls,
               A requiem among earth's souls.

The flag hung drooping from the masts,
   Faint echoes come and go and die,
      Tears fill the eyes welled from the past,
         Of those who see a comrade lie
            Where memory must be a name,
               And tablets praise a hero's frame.

What then? A soldier gives his life,
   For love of country valorous deeds,
      And lies as one whom carnal strife
         Marked for its own among its seeds.
            Ah, yes! Ere yet a flashing blade
               Was drawn or sheathed his grave was made.

Who calls the names of those to fall?
   Ask of the God of battles, who?
      But they are known. And some of all
         Who go to war to dare to do
            Know that the piercing shot will bring
            To him his altar's offering.

– Continued –

SEVENTY-SEVEN YEARS IN DIXIE

Some meet the shock within the fray,
   Some fall within the nurses' tent maintained.
      Weak and gaunt they waste away,
         Yet to its end each way is bent;
            The end? Deserved promotion calls
               To higher life each one that falls.

                              (AUTHOR UNKNOWN)
                              SELECTED BY LILLA GUNN
                              SANTA ROSA, FLORIDA

ABOUT THE EDITOR

Karen Schansman is a native of Wichita, Kansas. She was one of the founders and served on the board of the South Walton Three Arts Alliance in Walton County, Florida for three years. Karen served on the editorial staff and contributed articles for the Three Art Alliance's two historical books, *The Way We Were: Recollections of South Walton Pioneers* and *Of Days Gone By: Reflections of South Walton County, Florida*. In addition to editing this volume, Karen has edited *This Is My Life* by Walker H. Reddick Sr. Karen and her husband Terry live on Hewett Bayou off the Choctawhatchee Bay a few miles from the homestead of Henry Reddick on Four Mile Point.

ABOUT THE ILLUSTRATOR

Nancy R. Voith is a native of Maryland, but her twenty-six years of residing in Texas have influenced her artwork by offering numerous opportunities for professional study and artistic inspiration. She currently lives half of the year in Nashville and the other half in Santa Rosa Beach. Her work has been featured in numerous national juried shows in thirteen states. Harmony Farms Antiques and Gallery in Pulaski, Tennessee is currently offering several of her paintings. Nancy's favorite media are watercolor, pastels, and ink.

Made in the USA
Middletown, DE
30 September 2016